OUR
GRE★T
STATES

WHAT'S GREAT ABOUT
GEORGIA?

✳ Andrea Wang

⌊ LERNER PUBLICATIONS COMPANY ✳ MINNEAPOLIS

CONTENTS

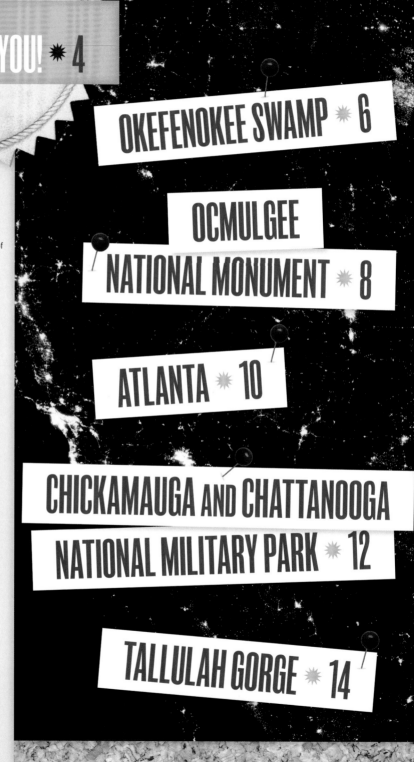

GEORGIA WELCOMES YOU! ✳ 4

Content Consultant: David Parker, Professor of History, Kennesaw State University

Lerner Publications Company
A division of Lerner Publishing Group, Inc.
241 First Avenue North
Minneapolis, MN 55401 USA

For reading levels and more information, look up this title at www.lernerbooks.com.

Main body text set in ITC Franklin Gothic Std Book Condensed 12/15.
Typeface provided by Adobe Systems.

Library of Congress Cataloging-in-Publication Data

Wang, Andrea.
     What's great about Georgia? / by Andrea Wang.
          pages cm. — (Our great states)
     Includes index.
     ISBN 978-1-4677-3337-3 (lib. bdg. : alk. paper)
     ISBN 978-1-4677-4709-7 (eBook)
     1. Georgia—Juvenile literature. I. Title.
F286.3.W36 2015
975.8—dc23   2013050866

Manufactured in the United States of America
1 – PC – 7/15/14

GEORGIA Welcomes You!

Welcome to the Peach State. Georgia is the home of the three *P*s. It's known for peaches, pecans, and peanuts! The state has a great mix of large cities and small country towns. It also has an amazing landscape. You can hike mountains, cross gorges, and swim in the ocean. You can go boating, camping, and fishing. You'll never even have to cross the state line! The state also has a rich history. Georgia played an important part in the American Revolutionary War (1775–1783) and the Civil War (1861–1865). Georgia is well known for its super-friendly people. Read on to learn ten things that make Georgia great. Then drop by for a slice of peach cobbler and a cool glass of sweet tea!

BLUE RIDGE MOUNTAINS

NORTH CAROLINA

Brasstown Bald
(4,784 feet/1,458 m)

Dalton

Gainesville

Chattahoochee River

Savannah River

Athens

Atlanta

Augusta

SOUTH CAROLINA

ALABAMA

Macon

Oconee River

Warner Robins

Columbus

Flint River

Savannah

Altamaha River

ATLANTIC OCEAN

Albany

N

Valdosta

Suwannee River

FLORIDA

Miles
0   20   40
0 20 40 60
Kilometers

Explore Georgia's cities and all the places in between! Just turn the page to find out all about the PEACH STATE. >

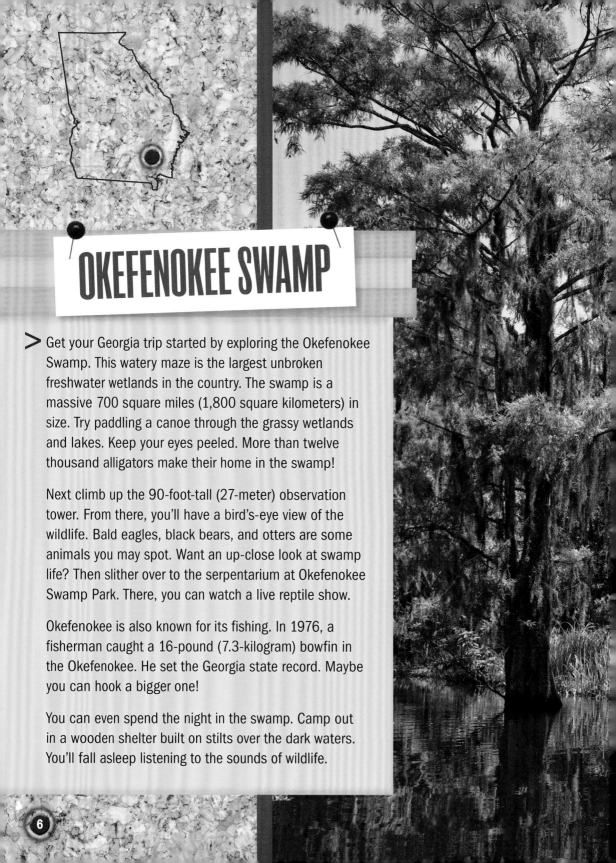

OKEFENOKEE SWAMP

> Get your Georgia trip started by exploring the Okefenokee Swamp. This watery maze is the largest unbroken freshwater wetlands in the country. The swamp is a massive 700 square miles (1,800 square kilometers) in size. Try paddling a canoe through the grassy wetlands and lakes. Keep your eyes peeled. More than twelve thousand alligators make their home in the swamp!

Next climb up the 90-foot-tall (27-meter) observation tower. From there, you'll have a bird's-eye view of the wildlife. Bald eagles, black bears, and otters are some animals you may spot. Want an up-close look at swamp life? Then slither over to the serpentarium at Okefenokee Swamp Park. There, you can watch a live reptile show.

Okefenokee is also known for its fishing. In 1976, a fisherman caught a 16-pound (7.3-kilogram) bowfin in the Okefenokee. He set the Georgia state record. Maybe you can hook a bigger one!

You can even spend the night in the swamp. Camp out in a wooden shelter built on stilts over the dark waters. You'll fall asleep listening to the sounds of wildlife.

You might see otters *(left)* or alligators *(below)* lurking in the dense wetlands of Okefenokee Swamp.

OCMULGEE NATIONAL MONUMENT

> People have called Georgia home for thousands of years. The Creek American Indians built huge dirt mounds in Georgia. The mounds are thousands of years old. You can still visit some of these mounds at the Ocmulgee National Monument in Macon. The Great Temple Mound soars 90 feet (27 m) above the Ocmulgee River. Climb the stairs to the top. Then take in the striking view of the Ocmulgee River valley.

There's plenty more to do at Ocmulgee. You can run, walk, or bike the miles of trails that lead to six other mounds. Make sure to swing by the visitor's center. It has cool collections of arrowheads and pottery on display. People found these objects at Ocmulgee. You can even make your own clay pot to take home.

In September, meet American Indians from many nations at the Ocmulgee Indian Celebration. Show off your moves in a friendship dance. You'll have the chance to sing traditional songs. You can even learn to play stickball, a traditional American Indian game.

CREEK LIFE

The Creek American Indians once lived in small towns across much of Georgia and Alabama. Each town had a central plaza. This was a gathering place. The Creek farmed corn, squash, and beans. They also hunted. The mounds the Creek built at Ocmulgee had many uses. Religious temples topped the two largest mounds. The Creek used the Funeral Mound to bury their dead.

Peek inside a replica of a Creek earth lodge at Ocmulgee National Monument.

9

ATLANTA

> Atlanta is full of fun things to do! It is the largest city in Georgia and also the capital. Atlanta is home to museums, parks, and theaters.

If you love animals, be sure to visit Zoo Atlanta. It has endangered gorillas, red pandas, and black rhinos. You'll feel like a deep-sea explorer at the Georgia Aquarium. Here, you can walk through an underwater tunnel. The tunnel has clear walls. Thousands of fish swim all around you. Get up close with massive manta rays and giant whale sharks.

Seeing all that water might make you thirsty. If so, just head next door to World of Coca-Cola. The famous soda was invented in Atlanta in 1886. This exhibition highlights the history of Coca-Cola. Give your taste buds a workout at the Coca-Cola Freestyle machine. This soda fountain offers more than one hundred types of drinks. They come from all around the world. Then head downstairs to see the vault where the makers of Coca-Cola keep the secret recipe!

CIVIL RIGHTS LEADER

Atlanta was an important city in the civil rights movement. The movement took place in the 1950s and the 1960s. Atlanta native Dr. Martin Luther King Jr. was one of the best-known leaders of the civil rights movement. He fought hard for equal treatment for African Americans. He dreamed of a peaceful world where all people were treated fairly. Visit the Martin Luther King Jr. National Historic Site in Atlanta. There, you can see the house where he was born.

The secret recipe for Coca-Cola is hidden in a carefully guarded vault at the World of Coca-Cola.

CHICKAMAUGA AND CHATTANOOGA NATIONAL MILITARY PARK

> Chickamauga and Chattanooga National Military Park is the largest military park in the country. The park was built to honor the Civil War battles of Chickamauga and Chattanooga in 1863.

Hop on a bike to explore the park. Can you find eight pyramids made out of cannonballs? The pyramids honor Civil War commanders in the Union and Confederate armies. Climb the 85-foot-tall (26 m) Wilder Brigade Monument. Don't forget to take a picture of the riderless horse monument nearby. This is the most photographed monument in the park.

Park rangers offer guided tours. They will tell you all about the battles that took place nearby. You can also watch musket and artillery demonstrations.

The city of Chickamauga is near the military park. Each year, Chickamauga hosts the War Between the States Day festival. You can watch people reenact the Battle of Chickamauga.

THE CIVIL WAR

In the Civil War, the Southern Confederacy fought to separate from the Northern Union. Georgia was in the Confederacy. Slavery was one of the main issues between the North and the South. Most people in the North were against slavery. Most white people in the South supported it. In 1865, the Confederate armies surrendered to the Union. The United States reunited and slavery ended.

A park volunteer *(left)* teaches visitors how to load a Civil War cannon during the 149th anniversary of the Battle of Chickamauga.

In the hot Georgia summer, a dip in the waters of Tallulah Lake is a great way to cool off after a hike.

TALLULAH GORGE

> Tallulah Gorge is one of the most exciting natural wonders in Georgia. By day, it is a gorgeous, 1,000-foot-deep (305 m) canyon. But night visits offer maximum thrills. Follow your guide on a nighttime hike down to the suspension bridge. The full moon will light your way. Hang on tight! The bridge bounces and sways 80 feet (24 m) above the roaring Hurricane Falls.

After your hike, you can camp at one of the park's campsites. The next day, enjoy lunch at a picnic shelter. Swim at the beach on Tallulah Lake. Go mountain biking on one of the area's many trails. You can even test your skill with a bow and arrow at the gorge's archery range.

The swinging suspension bridge at Tallulah Gorge is one of the park's many highlights.

DAHLONEGA MINING TOWN

> The first gold rush in the country took place at Dahlonega. Legend says a hunter named Benjamin Parks first found gold there in 1828. Parks tripped over a rock near Dahlonega. But it was no ordinary rock. It was full of gold! Soon approximately fifteen thousand treasure hunters flooded the town.

You can still visit this quaint mining town. Catch gold fever at the Dahlonega Gold Museum. Even the brick walls glitter with flecks of gold. The museum features a shiny gold nugget. Gleaming rare coins are also on display. Travel 120 feet (37 m) down into the earth at the Consolidated Gold Mine. See the tools Dahlonega's miners used. Then you can explore 5 miles (8 km) of underground tunnels.

In the fall, celebrate Dahlonega's history at Gold Rush Days. This two-day festival features hog calling. You also can try buck dancing. This is a type of clogging. You can even take part in a gold-panning contest!

In 1828, many miners came to Dahlonega with the hope of turning up gold nuggets.

Learn how to pan for gold at the Consolidated Gold Mine in Dahlonega.

SAVANNAH

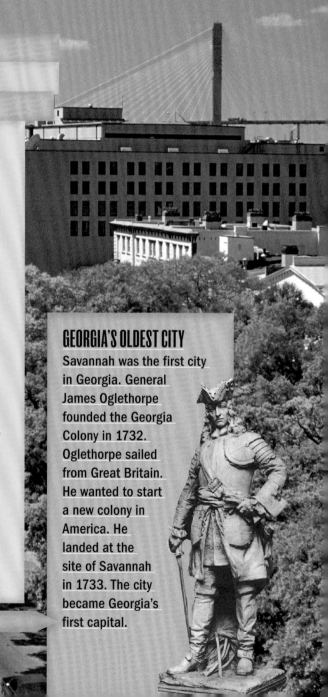

> Savannah is full of friendly people. In fact, it's known as the Hostess City. Start your visit with a scavenger hunt by Savannah Fun Tours. Find all the items on your list. You'll see exciting city landmarks at the same time.

Then celebrate Georgia's first railroad at the Georgia State Railroad Museum. Find out how to turn trains around in the roundhouse. Climb aboard old train cars. You can even take a ride on an old stream train.

Ships were an important part of Savannah's history. And sometimes pirates sailed into town! Grab some grub at the Pirates' House restaurant. Bloodthirsty buccaneers hung out here in the 1700s. After dinner, give yourself goose bumps on one of Savannah's many ghost tours. Some folks say Savannah is one of the most haunted cities in the United States!

GEORGIA'S OLDEST CITY

Savannah was the first city in Georgia. General James Oglethorpe founded the Georgia Colony in 1732. Oglethorpe sailed from Great Britain. He wanted to start a new colony in America. He landed at the site of Savannah in 1733. The city became Georgia's first capital.

Savannah's Colonial Park Cemetery, built in 1750, is a popular stop for many ghost tours. Some people say it's one of the most haunted places in the city!

STONE MOUNTAIN PARK

> Stone Mountain Park is the most popular place to visit in the state. It's easy to see why! This huge adventure park has fun for everyone.

Don't miss the Summit Skyride. This cable car takes you 825 feet (251 m) to the top of Stone Mountain. From there, you can see the Atlanta skyline nearly 20 miles (32 km) away. On the way up, you'll see the biggest granite sculpture in the world. It shows three Confederate leaders from the Civil War.

Head back down the mountain to get soaked by the shooting geyser. Geyser Towers is both a water park and a playground. You can scramble through net tunnels. Dart across the many platforms. Try to dodge the water if you can!

There is plenty to do for people who would rather stay high and dry. Test your balance on the Sky Hike. This treetop ropes course has net bridges and swinging ropes. The tallest part is four stories high. Then come back to earth with a round of miniature golf.

Take in the breathtaking scenery as you ride the cable car up to Stone Mountain's summit.

The carving on Stone Mountain shows Confederate president Jefferson Davis *(left)* and Generals Robert E. Lee *(center)* and Thomas Jonathan "Stonewall" Jackson *(right)*.

CALLAWAY PLANTATION

> Georgia may be known for its peaches, pecans, and peanuts, but an old saying in Georgia claims that "Cotton is King." Indeed, at one time, cotton was the state's most important crop. Learn more about cotton at Callaway Plantation in Washington, Georgia.

The estate is more than two hundred years old. It was once a working cotton plantation owned by the Callaway family. Now, the city of Washington has turned it into a museum. You can explore a blacksmith's house. Or visit a schoolhouse and a weaving house. Children's toys from long ago are on display. You can even pick your own fluffy, white cotton bolls.

In October, make sure to stop by for the Mule Day Southern Heritage Festival. You'll learn how to spin yarn, make candles, and weave on a loom. But don't forget the stars of the show! Cheer on your favorite in the mule contests. See which mule is the best plower. Then try using a mule to plow a straight line. It's harder than it looks!

JIMMY CARTER

Jimmy Carter started out as a humble peanut farmer from Plains, Georgia. In 1977, he became the thirty-ninth president of the United States! Later, Carter worked on global peacekeeping efforts. In 2002, he received the Nobel Peace Prize.

Cotton is still one of Georgia's most important crops.

CENTENNIAL OLYMPIC PARK

> Georgia is one of only five US states to have hosted the Olympic Games. Atlanta was the site of the 1996 Summer Olympics. Centennial Olympic Park is still a fun place to visit. Boogie to the beat at the Fountain of Rings. The fountain has water jets in the shape of the Olympic rings. The jets shoot water in time to music.

In the summer, you can buy lunch at the farmers' market. Then have a picnic on the Great Lawn. Bring a Frisbee or a football to toss around afterward. In the winter, the park offers skating on the outdoor ice rink. The park is lit up with holiday lights.

End your day with a ride on the SkyView Atlanta Ferris wheel. You'll get to see the city from 200 feet (61 m) in the air.

YOUR TOP TEN

You've read about ten awesome things to see and do in Georgia. Now think about what your Georgia top ten list would include. Imagine you are planning a trip to Georgia. What would you like to see if you visited the state? What would you like to do there? Keep these questions in mind as you make your own top ten list. Write your top ten list on a sheet of paper. You can even turn your list into a book. Illustrate it with drawings or with pictures from the Internet or magazines.

Sculptures in Centennial Olympic Park honor the 1996 Olympic Games, which took place there.

GEORGIA BY MAP

> MAP KEY

⭐ Capital city

○ City

◎ Point of interest

▲ Highest elevation

—·— State border

Visit www.lerneresource.com to learn more about the state flag of Georgia.

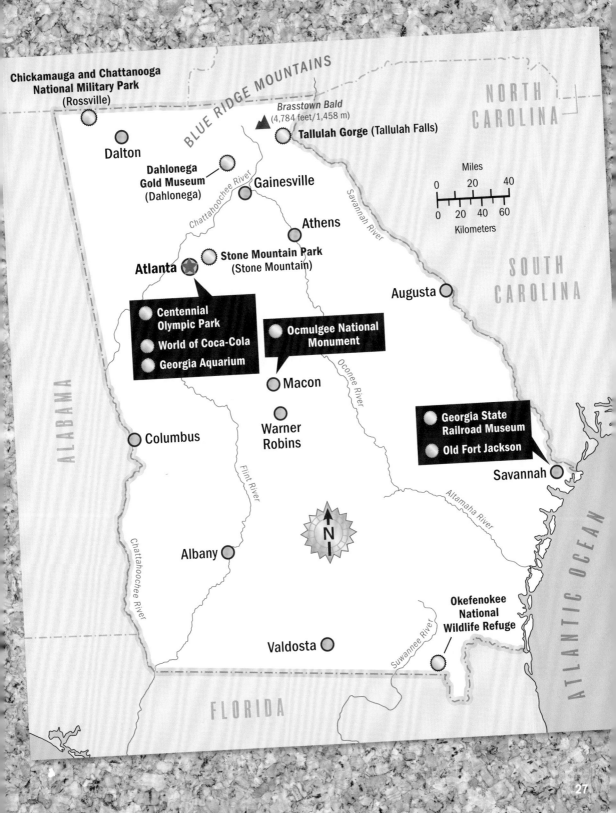

Chickamauga and Chattanooga
National Military Park
(Rossville)

BLUE RIDGE MOUNTAINS

NORTH
CAROLINA

Brasstown Bald
(4,784 feet/1,458 m)
▲ Tallulah Gorge (Tallulah Falls)

Dalton

Dahlonega
Gold Museum
(Dahlonega)

Chattahoochee River

Gainesville

Savannah River

Miles
0   20   40
0   20   40   60
Kilometers

Athens

Atlanta

Stone Mountain Park
(Stone Mountain)

SOUTH
CAROLINA

Augusta

Centennial
Olympic Park

World of Coca-Cola

Georgia Aquarium

Ocmulgee National
Monument

Oconee River

Macon

Warner
Robins

Georgia State
Railroad Museum

Old Fort Jackson

ALABAMA

Columbus

Flint River

Altamaha River

Savannah

N

Albany

Chattahoochee River

Okefenokee
National
Wildlife Refuge

ATLANTIC OCEAN

Valdosta

Suwannee River

FLORIDA

27

GEORGIA FACTS

NICKNAMES: Peach State, Empire State of the South

SONG: "Georgia on My Mind" by Stuart Gorrell and Hoagy Carmichael

MOTTO: "Wisdom, Justice, and Moderation"

FLOWER: Cherokee rose

> **TREE:** live oak

BIRD: brown thrasher

> **ANIMALS:** gopher tortoise, green tree frog, largemouth bass

> **FOODS:** peach, peanut, Vidalia onion

DATE AND RANK OF STATEHOOD: January 2, 1788; the 4th state

> **CAPITAL:** Atlanta

AREA: 58,921 square miles (152,605 sq. km)

AVERAGE JANUARY TEMPERATURE: 46°F (7.8°C)

AVERAGE JULY TEMPERATURE: 80°F (27°C)

POPULATION AND RANK: 9,919,945; 8th (2012)

MAJOR CITIES AND POPULATION: Atlanta (443,775), Columbus (198,413), Augusta (197,872), Savannah (142,022), Athens (118,999)

NUMBER OF US CONGRESS MEMBERS: 14 representatives, 2 senators

NUMBER OF ELECTORAL VOTES: 16

NATURAL RESOURCES: clay, coal, copper, fish, game, gravel, iron ore, kaolin, lumber, manganese, marble, oil, sand, stone

AGRICULTURAL PRODUCTS: cattle, cotton, dairy products, eggs, peaches, peanuts, poultry, vegetables, Vidalia onions

MANUFACTURED GOODS: chemical products, electric equipment, paper products, textiles and apparel, transportation equipment

STATE HOLIDAYS: Robert E. Lee's Birthday, Confederate Memorial Day

GLOSSARY

artillery: large guns that can shoot long distances

boll: the pod that contains a cotton plant's seeds. Its white hairs can be used to make cloth.

crop: a plant that can be grown and harvested

exhibition: a public display of interesting items

geyser: a spring that shoots water and steam

gorge: a narrow passage, ravine, or steep-walled canyon

musket: an old-fashioned gun once used by soldiers

plaza: an open public area that can be used as a gathering place

quaint: old-fashioned and charming

reenact: to act or perform the actions of an earlier event

summit: the highest point of a mountain

surrender: to give up and stop fighting

vault: a room or safe used to store and protect valuable objects

FURTHER INFORMATION

Awesome America: Georgia
http://awesomeamerica.com/georgia
This website has tons of information to help you plan your trip to Georgia, plus many beautiful photos.

Cunningham, Kevin. *The Georgia Colony*. New York: Scholastic, 2011. Experience the true adventures of men and women who founded the thirteenth colony, Georgia.

deRubertis, Barbara. *Let's Celebrate Martin Luther King Jr. Day*. New York: Kane Press, 2013. Read about the life and work of Atlanta's Martin Luther King Jr.

Georgia Facts, Map, and State Symbols
http://www.enchantedlearning.com/usa/states/georgia
Visit this site to learn more about the Peach State. It has many facts, maps, and fun activities about Georgia.

Georgia for Kids
http://www.ipl.org/div/stateknow/ga1.html
Check out facts, figures, and an awesome set of web links that take you to all the information you want to know about Georgia.

Jerome, Kate Boehm. *Savannah and the State of Georgia: Cool Stuff Every Kid Should Know*. Charleston, SC: Arcadia Publishing, 2011. This fun book is full of fascinating facts about the first capital city of Georgia, Savannah.

INDEX

PHOTO ACKNOWLEDGMENTS

The images in this book are used with the permission of: © Sean Pavone/Shutterstock Images, p. 1; © D'Vine Photography/Shutterstock Images, p. 4; © Rudolf Balasko/Thinkstock, pp. 4–5; © Laura Westlund/Independent Picture Service, pp. 5 (top), 26–27; © Barbara Kraus /Thinkstock, pp. 6–7; © Brian Lasenby /Shutterstock Images, p. 7 (left); © KAdams66 /Thinkstock, p. 7 (right); © age fotostock /SuperStock, pp. 8–9; © Prisma/SuperStock, p. 9 (bottom); Library of Congress, pp. 9 (top) (LC-USZC4-2952), 18 (LC-USZ62-61452); © Rudy Balasko/Shutterstock Images, pp. 10–11; Dick DeMarsico/Library of Congress, p. 10 (LC-USZ62-122988); © David Goldman/AP Images, p. 11; © National Park Service/AP Images, pp. 12–13; © North Wind/North Wind Picture Archives, p. 12; © Allison Love /Chattanooga Times Free Press/AP Images, p. 13; © SeanPavonePhoto/Shutterstock Images, pp. 14–15; © Ron Buskirk/Alamy, p. 14; © ciapix /Shutterstock Images, p. 15; © Ian Dagnall/Alamy, pp. 16–17; © Marcel Clemens/Glow Images, p. 17 (left); © Oliver Gerhard/Glow Images, p. 17 (right); © spirit of america/Shutterstock Images, pp. 18–19; © David Davis/Shutterstock Images, p. 19; © kurdistan/Shutterstock Images, pp. 20–21; © jcarillet/iStockphoto, p. 21 (left); © Shawn Zhang/Shutterstock Images, p. 21 (right); © Denton Rumsey/Shutterstock Images, pp. 22–23; Karl Schumacher/Library of Congress, p. 22 (LC-USZC4-599); © Katherine Welles /Shutterstock Images, p. 23; © Rob Hainer /Shutterstock Images, pp. 24–25; © L. Kragt Bakker/Shutterstock Images, p. 25; © Paul Stringer/Shutterstock Images, p. 26; © John Keith/Shutterstock Images, p. 29 (top); © Charles Gibson/Thinkstock, p. 29 (middle top); © moodboard/Thinkstock, p. 29 (middle bottom); © J. Waldron/Shutterstock Images, p. 29 (bottom).

Cover: © Duane Miller/Getty Images (trees); © iStockphoto.com/Pannonia (peaches); © Sean Pavone/Shutterstock.com (Atlanta, GA); © Jeffrey M. Frank/Shutterstock.com (cannon); © Laura Westlund/Independent Picture Service (map); © iStockphoto.com/fpm (seal); © iStockphoto .com/vicm (pushpins); © iStockphoto.com /benz190 (corkboard).